ISBN 978-1-333-74380-2
PIBN 10542132

English
Français
Deutsche
Italiano
Español
Português

www.forgottenbooks.com

Mythology Photography **Fiction**
Fishing Christianity **Art** Cooking
Essays Buddhism Freemasonry
Medicine **Biology** Music **Ancient**
Egypt Evolution Carpentry Physics
Dance Geology **Mathematics** Fitness
Shakespeare **Folklore** Yoga Marketing
Confidence Immortality Biographies
Poetry **Psychology** Witchcraft
Electronics Chemistry History **Law**
Accounting **Philosophy** Anthropology
Alchemy Drama Quantum Mechanics
Atheism Sexual Health **Ancient History**
Entrepreneurship Languages Sport
Paleontology Needlework Islam
Metaphysics Investment Archaeology
Parenting Statistics Criminology
Motivational

CHRISTIANITY, THE ONLY RELIGION FOR MAN.

A DISCOURSE

DELIVERED BEFORE THE

GRADUATING CLASS

OF THE

UNIVERSITY OF NORTH CAROLINA,

JUNE 4, 1855.

BY B. M. PALMER, D. D.,
COLUMBIA, S. C.

RALEIGH:
PRINTED AT THE OFFICE OF THE "CAROLINA CULTIVATOR."

1855.

UNIVERSITY CHAPEL, CHAPEL HILL, N. C., ·
June 5th, 1855.

DEAR SIR:—You will please accept the sincere thanks of the Graduating Class, for the interesting Sermon, addressed to us, last evening, in this house.

It is but little, that we acknowledge our more than satisfaction, and high appreciation of the effort, allow us to say, that we are not contented to have heard once, so learned and masterly a discourse, which convinced us so thoroughly of the *Truth* of Christianity ; but, we desire to turn over its pages ourselves, and offer to others the same privilege. We would, therefore, respectfully solicit a copy for publication.

Adding our own earnest solicitation to that of the class, and hoping you may see fit to comply with our request, we beg leave to sign ourselves,

Your humble serv'ts,

JAS. H. COLTON,
JAS. PARK,
D. E. McNAIR,
Committee of the Grad. Class.

Rev. B. M. Palmer, D. D.

———

CHAPEL HILL, N. C., June 5, 1855.

To Messrs. J. H. COLTON *and others, Committee,*

GENTLEMEN—I herewith place in your hands, the Discourse delivered on last evening, hoping and praying that its serious perusal may, by the Divine Spirit, be blessed to those for whom it was prepared.

With sincere reciprocation of the kindly sentiments you have so gratefully expressed in your note,

I am, Gentlemen,
Very truly yours,

B. M. PALMER.

SERMON.

JOHN vi. 68, 69.

"THEN SIMON PETER ANSWERED HIM, LORD, TO WHOM SHALL WE GO."
"THOU HAST THE WORDS OF ETERNAL LIFE: AND WE BELIEVE AND
ARE SURE THAT THOU ART THAT CHRIST, THE SON OF THE LIVING
GOD."

The miracle of feeding five thousand men with
five barley loaves, was one so practical and use-
ful, that the despairing patriotism of the Jews was
suddenly revived. The spirit of sturdy independ-
ence nourished through fifteen hundred years of a
supernatural and sacred history, but which had
chafed under nearly six centuries of tributary sub-
jection, was now panting for a deliverer, as
when the cry of their Fathers went up to Heaven under the oppressions of Egypt. Might not
this wonder-working prophet again judge Israel
with such deeds as when the rams' horns of Joshua
blew down the walls of Jericho: or when the com-
panies of Gideon broke their pitchers against the
camp of the Midianites? And with such a cham-
pion might not the rainbow of the ancient glory

such thoughts, tracking the Saviour's mysterious
path across the sea of Galilee, the excited patriots

were soon to learn that His kingdom " was
meat and drink, but righteousness, and peace,
joy in the Holy Ghost." " Labour not for the n
which perisheth, but for that meat which endu
unto everlasting life, which the Son of Man s
give unto you; for Him hath God the Father s
ed." This plain language, the only answer wl
is returned to their ambitious proposal, the J
with all their bias, could not well mistake. Tl
evidently understood Christ as professing to fo
a new and spiritual dispensation; and requiring
other systems to be renounced, not excepting
daism itself. As they filed away in disappointm
and anger, He who came to His own saw w
sorrow His own receiving him not; and turn
with deepest pathos in His tone, He said unto
twelve, " Will ye also go away?" With t
characteristic ardour which made him always
speaker of the Apostolic College, Peter replies
"·Lord, to whom shall we go? Thou hast the wo
of eternal life." He means to say in behalf of
colleagues and himself, that they adhere to Ch
upon the very grounds on which others deser
him, because He was " the true God and Eter
Life.' Religious wants were developed in th

" that · Christ, · the son of the · living· God." 7
choice with · them lay · not · between religion ε

atheism; for a religion they must have, and the alternative was either of the true or the false. Upon a deliberate survey of all systems, both of philosophy and religion, christianity alone was found to solve their doubts and to satisfy their wants.

Young gentlemen, you have seen in the Camera a broad landscape of lake and forest lie, in beautiful though diminished proportions, upon a sheet of paper. It is so with the text. Here in the pregnant reply of Peter is found an argument, which covers the whole breadth of our nature.— His rapid interrogation, "to whom shall we go," confesses man's need of a divinely extracted religion. His affirmation reveals the essential conditions it must fulfil, in teaching "the words of eternal life." I propose now to fill up this bold outline with well-considered proofs of these two points:

I.—*That man's religious nature constrains him to find repose in some form of faith and worship.*

II.—*That the wants of this nature, well understood, are met only in Christianity, as taught in the Gospel.*

I shall dwell chiefly upon the second proposition; though the first merits attention as antecedently the ground-form of the other. It would evidently be supererogatory to discuss the pre-eminent fitness of any one religious scheme, if men can dispense with all schemes alike. The question then recurs:

I.—*Has man a religious nature which compels him to the faith and worship of God?* To answer this question, let us consider—

1. *The elements which enter into our own moral constitution.* Take *conscience*, for example. Without entering into abstract discussion of the nature of conscience—whether it be an independent and single faculty, or only a name given to the complex operation of all our powers, when directed to moral subjects—upon any view, it is that department of our nature which makes us cognizant of law. As the understanding distinguishes between the true and the false, and as the taste discriminates between the beautiful and the vile, so conscience authoritatively decides between the right and the wrong. Now the question arises, what is the original ground of these moral distinctions, the source from which they spring? Evidently, the theory of Hobbes does not exhaust the inquiry, that they are entirely the creatures of human prudence, and have their foundation in human legislation. It is sufficient to reply, that human law is itself a creation, and can suggest nothing beyond the contents of the lawgiver's own mind. In tracing a stream to its source, the navigator will not pause thus at what is at best only the mouth of a single tributary. We

are yet to be told how these moral distinctions first occurred to the legislator, to be impressed upon his code; and how, when suggested by him, they should obtain so uniformly among men, as never yet happened with any institutes that were purely arbitrary. If, then, we discover these operations of conscience to be universal, and can trace them in an ascending series above all human legislation, nothing remains but to insist upon all morality as eternal and immutable, existing ab extra, anterior to all earthly enactments; and though requiring human relations as the sphere of its operation, yet having its ground in something far higher and more enduring. We have exhausted all analysis, when we refer it directly to the infinitely holy nature of God; and make the divine will, however revealed—whether in written statutes, or engraved upon our moral constitution—its ultimate standard. Since man was created originally in Jehovah's image, the divine law was stamped upon his nature, the essential condition of his moral activity, just as the atmosphere is the condition of life. To this law the conscience has respect in all its judgments, as the exponant of that morality of which the divine nature is the ground. Thus, if Conscience be a witness, sealing up its testimony to the Great Assize, its depositions state the contrariety or agreement of human conduct with the precepts of this law. If it be a judge, sitting upon God's lower tribunal in the soul, its decisions are but the interpretations of the same law. If it be a rule, it only proximately reveals the contents of that primary law. Nor does it affect the integrity of this argument, that Conscience, as a witness, is often corrupted by interest; as a judge, is biassed by passion; and as a rule, is perverted by prejudice. Blinded by ignorance, defiled by sin, and paralyzed by resistance, it is still an indestructible element of our nature. Mistaken often in her judgments, decisions she does render; incorrect in her interpretations of the law, expositions she will give; and though drugged by opiates into occasional repose, the torments of the lost show she has power to awake, and take ample reprisals for the wrong. If Conscience, then, be this organ of an original law impressed upon the soul, every response is a witness for God; and every moral judgment is an oracle bidding man find his satisfaction only in a divine fellowship.

Precisely the same line of argument might be pursued with any other element of our moral constitution, say *the affections.* It is as natural for man to love, as to breathe or to think; and he does the one or the other by the uncontrollable necessity of his being. If he lock up his affections within his own breast, he pays the forfeit of disobedience to the social law of the universe in a blighted nature, mildewing beneath the lichen and moss which cover its ruins. It is the peculiar property of love however, that it carries itself unbroken and entire, to each object lying within a given circle. It is not something parcelled out in measure to each, until the whole is exhausted; but flowing forth in a perennial stream, the volume is never diminished by the extent of its distribution. Thus the parent bestows upon every child, the entire wealth of his love; each having the whole, though it is shared by several.* Nor do the human affections, like the waters of the Nile, overflow only a single Delta, but are distributed over all the relationships of life, lying as these do in concentric circles; so that the whole undivided heart is carried over from one circle to another, until all are embraced in one comprehensive fellowship. What do the expansiveness and unity of our affections prove, but that when we have loved through the entire breadth of earthly relations, the undiminished heart remains to pour its treasures into the bosom of a Being higher and nobler than ourselves? As it sweeps inward with increasing intensity of love within each narrower circle, should it pause in its path until it rests upon the great I Am, who is the common centre of them all? Each radius of every circle in human society

---

* This thought is presented in Taylor's Spiritual Christianity.

conducts the heart to that central Being fror
whom all others spring, and around whose thron
all human orbits are described.

I must be content with merely sketching th
outline of an argument, which cannot · be _fi¹le'
up without expanding this discourse into a treatis(
But you will readily see how the argument migh
be conducted from *the intellectual powers*, feelin;
onward through all nature to God, who is the sun
and source of all knowledge. And how again *the ac
tive powers* should find their rest and exercise alikε
in obeying that Sovereign will which moves th(
whole machinery of the universe. But these sid(
glances are sufficient to reveal that, place ourselve
at what point we may, in that moral constitution w·
possess, not a single element but has a separatι
voice for God; and whose passionate yearnings finι
no adequate expression, but in the language of ador
ing worship.

2. *The existence òf a religious nature may be infer
red from the tenacity with which religious ideas, onc
communicated, are retained by the mind.* ·The ne
cessary existence of God, His moral government, th(
holiness and immutability of His law, lie at the ba
sis of all religion. ·It is remarkable, that whateve:
be the source of our knowledge upon these points
they are accepted upon the first statement, and·caɪ
never afterwards be dislodged. Received, like th(

light, upon their own evidence, however capable of proof by reason, they do not depend upon argument for their propagation in the world. They seem to enter at once into the very texture of the mind; so that though overlaid, obscured, perverted, they are never forgotten nor erased. Thus, for example, while "the glory of the incorruptible God has been changed into an image, made like to corruptible man, and to birds, and to four-footed beasts, and to creeping things," yet the great idea itself of God's existence has never been eradicated. The very superstition which has multiplied the one living Jehovah into "Lords many and Gods many," and the idolatry which has attempted to symbolize and bring the Deity within the range of human thought, only show how originally cognate to the souls of men is the notion of a God. It would be easy to descend into a particular enumeration of religious opinions, which have resolutely maintained their dominion over the human conscience. The admission of man's sinfulness and consequent exposure to the divine curse, is expressed in the deprecatory rites of every false religion. The myths and legends, which form the oracles of Pagan antiquity, universally recognise God's conversableness with man, notwithstanding his apostasy. The incarnation of the Deity looms out in the numerous Avatars of the Hindoos, as well as in the anthropomor-

phic manifestations of the gods of classical myth(
ogy.   The altar-fires which have burned up(
every hill, lift up a universal testimony to the d(
trine of redemption by sacrifice.   Indeed, the
truths, broken off from an original revelation, ha'
intermingled themselves, fragmentary and distorte
with all the superstitions of men.   They have b
come interwoven with all their religious associatio1
and emotions; and though rendered grotesque b
the additions of a credulous superstition, they a1
nevertheless the archetypes of all those fables whic
describe God's commerce with mankind and contai
thus the essence even of Heathen religion.   Nov
could these truths command so universally the in
mediate assent of men, if there was not a suscept
bility for their reception ?   And to what but th
congeniality of a religious nature can we ascrit
the fact, that amidst a thousand distortions and ol
scurations, they have never yet been eliminate
from the human soul ?

3. But once for all: a conclusive argument fc
man's religious nature is found in *the universal pre1
alence of religion and worship in so many diverse form
over the globe*.   Man is no where without a religio1
Even in that savage state, where the attributes (
humanity are scarcely discovered, the traces of wo1
ship can be detected among the Bushmen and Ho1
tentots of Africa.   We perceive it equally in th

symbol-worship of ancient Egypt, in the fire-worship of ancient Persia, in the star-worship and divination of ancient Chaldea. We trace it in the dreamy contemplations of the Hindoo, seeking absorption into the pure being of Brahm; and in the mystical theism of the Buddhist, who seeks in the Grand Lama a glorified man who shall be the High Priest of the Universe, the central manifestation and representative of the Divine intelligence. We discover it in the old patriarchal faith of China, which makes social order the first principle of religion, and the Emperor the abiding representative of fatherly authority. It sparkles before us in the poetical mythology of classic Greece, whose beautiful conceptions, eschewing an abstract Divinity, transfigure men into Gods, presiding over all the departments of nature and forming a grand senate upon the top of Olympus. It clothes itself in the steel armour of ancient Rome, and sits upon the Capitol as a religion of Government and law. It utters itself in the wild battle cry of the Mahometan, claiming as his mission the practical assertion of a sovereign will ruling over the earth, which had nearly become obsolete amidst the theosophic speculations and idolatrous Image-worship of Christendom. Amidst the dark forests of Germany, the Goth worshipped the earth as his mother, and bowed before the God of the mist and the storm.

But I must not omit to mention what will strengtl
en my argument as much as it will awaken your a<
miration, the wonderful vitality of these anciei
faiths, inadequate as they seem to resist a violei
pressure from without. Buddhism, for exampl
passed over from Thibet and Burmah into Chin
and drove before it the cold state worship of Co:
fucius. But it could not entirely expel it: and no
the two religions with all their antitheses are see
side by side, dividing the homage of the Celestial En
pire. During five centuries the old Persian faith la
crushed and smothered under the Parthian dynast;
Yet it experienced at last a resurrection to powei
and the religion of Zoroaster, restored by the M
gians, connected the new kingdom with the old er
pire of Cyrus. Again it was overborne by the ster
proscription of Mahometan fanaticism; yet is it see
cropping out from the surface in an element of Pai
theism it has breathed into the doctrine of the K<
ran. In like manner, the dreamy Hindoo religio
now hoary with the lapse of thirty centuries, survive
the invasion of its kindred Buddhism; and thoug
again overlaid by the conquering creed of the Mu
sulman, its secret life was still preserved, survivin
merely by its own passive endurance. How shall thei
facts of history* be explained, unless these variou

---

* All of which have been taken from Maurice's " Religions of the World."

systems are admitted to contain some element of truth which finds an echo in the human soul? We stand nowhere upon this broad earth where a capacity for religion does not appear a characteristic of the race. Wherever we find the power of reason and the exercise of thought, we discover traces of the religious sentiment—often dark and gloomy, grotesque and wild, sensual and licentious, fanatical and bloody; yet sufficient to prove that man is, in the broad etymology of the term, a religious being.

The only exceptions, I confess at all perplexing, are those persons in Christian lands, who seem to live without any restraints of piety or forms of devotion; who enter no sanctuaries, and bow before no altars, and who speak only the language of profaneness and blasphemy. It is a portentous fact that the only men, who even in appearance are apostates from all religion, should be found in the heart of Christianity itself. Yet the strange paradox admits an easy solution. Where the forms of religion are such as suit the carnal taste, man is under no temptation to be a dissenter from the national worship. But where idolatry, in its Protean shapes, is excluded by the light of the Gospel, there is no resource for that carnal mind which is enmity against God but in this practical Atheism. Yet is it more apparent than real. The current religious opinions taken up

by absorption from the very atmosphere which the
breathe, are sufficient to preserve, even in these, tl
religious element from extinction. A close inves
gation would reveal that the most careless and pr
fane are not without a system of faith, more or le
extended and complete; and the religious instin
may perhaps find exercise in doubt and cavil as tr
ly as in belief and worship. Indeed these very pe
sons often exhibit most intensely the power of reli;
ion over the individual mind. Volney, meditatir
amidst the grey ruins of ancient Empires his assau
upon Christianity; Voltaire, composing at Ferney h
flippant diatribes which made him the Coryphœus
French Deists; Thomas Paine, retailing the filtl
scandal he had gathered from the bar-room and tl
barber shop; and David Hume, contravening as
philosopher those identical principles of human b
lief which as a historian he recognised; are all
them as striking instances of the power of religio
instinct, as the most zealous martyrs that ever ble
Religion truly maintains its ascendency as the mo
powerful element of our nature, when it asserts i
sway alike over those who resist, and over those wl
passively yield.

But I will not waste words in further elaborati
the proof of a position which perhaps you grant
me upon the bare statement. If then, young gentl
men, you heartily subscribe the belief that man

constrained by the imperious law of his nature to find repose in some form of faith and worship, I place you at once upon the panel before which Christianity shall to-night try her cause: and under the solemn sanction of an oath I bind you to render a true verdict, according to the evidence.

II. IT MUST NOW BE DEMONSTRATED TO YOU, THAT CHRISTIANITY HAS RESOURCES TO SATISFY THE DISTINCT AND ARTICULATE WANTS OF THIS NATURE.

1. *Consider then, that it is the only religion which presents to man a personal God, clothed with all the attributes of a perfect Being, with clearly revealed personal relations to the Creature.*

. Should we enter a common Sabbath School and propound the question, 'what is God,' a hundred slender voices would perhaps promptly reply in the language of the Westminster Catechism, "God is a spirit, infinite, eternal and unchangeable in his being wisdom, power, holiness, justice, goodness and truth." Now from this assemblage of perfections I might select one, and ask in what other religions does Holiness stand forth an essential property of the Gods whom they present as objects of worship? In vain do we consult the shasters of the Brahmin, the Zendavesta of the Magian, the Koran of the Mussulman, or the poetical legends of Ovid and Homer for an exhibition of that moral purity which enters into the most elementary Christian conception of the

Deity. I might tell you of the long process t
which this conception was transferred to the huma
mind, and wrought into human belief. How th
for three thousand years, the inspired prophet h;
stood side by side with the historian, pointing to tl
judgments with which an avenging providence h;
overtaken the transgressions of men, converting a
history into a discipline of this great truth, God
abhorrence of all impurity and sin. I might descrit
minutely that splendid Mosaic ritual given amid
lightning and tempest from the top of Sinai; its saci
fices, lustrations, and ablutions, creating a languag
of symbols to convey and express accurately to ma
the abstract idea of God's infinite holiness.* Bt
the waning moments warn me not to attempt an e:
haustive argument.

I must be content with asking where but in tl
Jehovah of the Scriptures do we find such a clust‹
of perfections as is set forth in this answer of our Sal
bath Scholar? If we pass through the Panthec
of Pagan Greece, the God within each separate nicl
is but the personification of a single attribute.-
Apollo, with his quiver and bow, embodies the co
ception of Wisdom; Venus, that of love; Mars, ‹
power; Bacchus, of inspiration; Chronos, devourin
his own offspring, of time stretching back into a

---

* See this well presented in an anonymous work entitled "Philosophy of t
Plan of Salvation."

untold and unreckoned duration; while Jupiter himself represents only the abstract notion of supremacy, or dominion. And when the acute Philosophy of Greece applied itself to the interpretation of these poetical Theogonies, and sought the deep and hidden ground out of which they sprung, even the Heirophants of the mysteries failed to combine these separate qualities into one complex conception; but lost themselves in the abyss of God's unfathomed being, or traced His manifestations only in a degrading pantheism.

But Christianity differs not less from all heathen religions in asserting the distinct personality of the supreme being. The term God in the Scriptures is not a mere envelope, binding into one complex conception these separate and abstract qualities, converting the Deity only into a bundle of attributes. The Bible presents Jehovah to our faith and worship as a personal being, of whose living nature these perfections may be predicated, and from which they are unfolded. When on the contrary we turn back to the religions of antiquity, we discover either the mythical popular faith, through the creations of the poets, deifying the powers of nature, and multiplying Gods until they shall equal all her diversified phenomena; or else the speculative spirit resolving all into a philosophical pantheism, in which the universe was viewed as a concrete deity, and

God was regarded only as the animating soul of n
ture. In both cases, the personality of God w;
lost, and He was hopelessly entangled with His un
verse. Nor is it better when we pass to the mo1
profound and speculative theosophy of the East.-
The Indian mystic is lost in the dream of compas
ing the absolute intelligence of Brahm or Buddl
and the Persian Magus is swallowed in the abyss
that illimitable Being, out of whom light and dar:
ness alike spring. How shall the Infinite pass o1
from the *Buthos* of His own essence into manifest
tion, and how shall he pass back again into pure b
ing? How shall the chasm be bridged between tl
Infinite and the finite? In vain does the orient
hypostatize the powers of Deity, and substitute li
ing personalities for abstract mental conceptions. I
has either peopled the universe with whole gener
tions of fantastic æons, or, his dualism resolves itse
into pantheistic manicheism. God is not a person
subsistence, but only a name given to the gener
notion of spirit; which becoming mysteriously c
agulated with matter, passes back through vario
stages of development and purification, until it
swallowed and lost in the abyss of the prim
essence again.

Here, then, does apologetic Christianity take h
first ground of defence. She presents to man t
living Jehovah as the object of worship: not t

personification of this or that single trait; not the deification of this or that power of nature; not a Pantheus wearing the universe as His outside garment; not the symbol merely of such abstract conceptions as absolute intelligence, or illimitable being, but a living, personal God, a spirit infinite and eternal, separate from matter, creating all things by the word of His power, and by whom all things consist. It is not simple being, and then it is Brahm; it is not pure intelligence, and then it is Buddh; it is not a destroyer, and then it is Siva; it is not a restorer, and then it is Vishna; it is not a malignant hater, and then it is Kali; it is not an arbitrary and mighty ruler, and then it is Allah; but it is the one living and true God, glorious in holiness, fearful in praises and doing wonders: one God, Father, Son and Holy Ghost, infinitely blessed in the communion of the Trinity, the living Jehovah, maker of Heaven and Earth, the creator, preserver, Redeemer; the lawgiver, ruler and judge, the everlasting father and unfailing portion of all who trust, and love, and worship him.

2. *Christianity is the only religion for man, since it alone reveals his true character and his future destiny.* What satisfactory accounts do Pagan theologians give of the human soul; who now consider it a spark emitted from the divine essence. and now regard it as matter in its most sublimated and ethe-

rial form ? Plato sought to establish, by probabl
reasoning, the soul's immortality ; yet with argu
ments so airy and unsubstantial that Cicero mourn
fully confesses they eluded his grasp, so soon as th
book containing them was laid aside. In what wa
the soul survives the shock of death, and whethe
in the world of spirits it will have an individua
subsistence as on earth, were left wholly unresolv
ed. The more positive and adventurous theosoph
of the East, gave a reply indeed, but a reply whicl
reduced all religion to emptiness and air. In thei
scheme, after countless transmigrations, the sou
was stripped of all limitation and individuality, an
merged into the substance of the Deity, as a drop o
water loses itself in the abyss of ocean.

While the Pagan conscience too, like Laocoon i
the embrace of the serpent, was writhing under
sense of the divine displeasure, what rational ex
planation was given of sin ? Blindly consciou
only of disruption from God, and of the power o
evil, their utterances were only the inarticulat
groans of a sick man under the oppression of frighl
ful dreams. Knowing nothing of a perfect mora
law, impressed upon us as the guide of our nature
which man, in the exercise of his freedom as a res
ponsible being had violated, sin was nothing bu
physical evil, arising from the soul's alliance witl
matter. Instead of being the corruption and defile

ment of the moral nature, it was only the thraldom of spirit in the fetters of material bondage. Redemption was only deliverance from this hateful alliance—the only purgation was metempsy chosis; and salvation but a name for final re-absorption into Deity. Their moral discipline of necessity, either diverged into a gloomy asceticism on the one hand, or else apostatized into lawless licentiousness on the other.

What light again did Pagan theology shed upon the awful mystery of death? What hand lifted the dark curtain which falls upon the stage of human life, showing whither the actors have fled? A little chattering nonsense of Charon and the river Styx, and the shades seen flitting through the gloom of Tartarus, is all that we find written upon the leaves of the ancient sibyl. When the sepulchral lamp revealed the body "clothed with all the dishonors of corruption," what heathen gospel " brought life and immortality to light?" The total ignorance which prevailed as to the resurrection of the body, vitiated the whole Heathen doctrine of a future state. Even Cicero, illuminated as he was with all the science and philosophy of antiquity, declared himself unable to conceive of embodied spirit And take away the retributions of a future world, what sanctions has religion with which to bind the consciences of men, putting her police into every hu-

man breast? "There is hope of a tree, if it be c
down, that it will sprout again, and through t
scent of water will bud and bring forth boughs li
a plant:" but which of the ancient augurs interpi
ted these analogies to the soul exclaiming in the to
ture of despair, "If a man die shall he live again
Socrates could say, when asked by Crito, how l
should be buried, "as you please, provided I do n
escape out of your hands," and enjoined upon l
friends not to mourn over his lifeless corpse, as if
were Socrates. And this was the highest reach
Heathen Divinity, to disown a part of one bein
and to the extent of one-half our nature, to consei
to certain annihilation. How much more thrillir
the language which the scripture put in the moul
of one who lived five centuries before Socrates, "M
flesh also shall rest in hope, for thou wilt not leav
my soul in hell, neither shall thy holy one see co
ruption; thou wilt show me the path of life, in tl
presence is fulness of joy, at thy right hand a
pleasures for evermore." Christianity reveals one
us, of whom these words were prophetically utte
ed a full millenium before his advent, one who
the Lord of the Resurrection, who has redeeme
both body and soul, and made them partakers
the same adoption; one who both died, and rose ar
revived, that he might be the Lord, both of the dea
and of the living; and who henceforward proclain

himself, in this royal style, "I am he that liveth and was dead, and behold I am alive forevermore, and have the keys of hell and death." A religion then, whose inspired voice authenticates such truths, discloses the real nature of that disease it designs to heal, and brings the distinct doctrine of a future state to sanction its claims, is beyond competition. And upon this ground does christianity challenge your verdict as the only true religion of man on earth.

3. In the third place, I present you the argument of Isaac Taylor, though in a different form, *that Christianity rests upon a historical basis ; it is a religion of facts.* The religions of antiquity, from first to last, were wrought in the forge of metaphysical speculation. Destitute of a written revelation, and with only a confused traditive remembrance of God's primitive manifestations to the race, they substituted fancies for facts, and reasoned rather than believed. Thus from age to age their cosmogonies were weaved with endless toil, mysteriously unravelled as fast as they were spun. Not content to know God, simply as the creator of the universe, they would determine *how* He is the author of all existence. Postulating a process of development in the very nature of Deity, they construed all existence to be an efflux from the Supreme being. The necessary result of grounding

all religion upon reason rather than faith is the i
troduction of an aristocratic element. The wc
shippers are divided into two classes; the initiat
or sacerdotal caste, whose theosophic speculatio.
are locked up in hieroglyphic and esoteric symbol
and the unelect masses who must be content with
mythical faith expressed in concrete and sensib
images. Thus was it ever impossible for these a
cient systems to embrace the race of man in a clo
religious brotherhood: and during six thousan
years the world has rocked uneasily between th
desperation of unbelief, giving it over a prey to si
perstition, and the irrationality of superstitio
driving it back to infidelity.

Now, in glowing contrast with all this, conside
the influence of Christianity as a religion of simpl
facts. It opens with the grand announcement tha
God is; and to all presumptuous inquiries into h
essence, the rebuke comes with a voice of thunde
from His pavilion, " Canst thou, by searching, fin
out God? Canst thou find out the Almighty unt
perfection? It is high as Heaven, what cans
thou do? Deeper than hell, what canst thou knov
the measure thereof is longer than the earth, an
broader than the sea." If men would inquire int
the generation of the universe, it turns the eye c
faith, beyond the whole series of outward phen
mena, to God's infinite power, and contemplat

creation as a great incomprehensible fact: "through faith we understand that the worlds were framed by the word of God, so that things which are seen, were not made of things which do appear." It does not suffer a metaphysical trinity like the Hindoo, Buddhist, or Platonic to be spun from human speculations, but baptizes us into the name of the one God, Father, Son and Holy Ghost. It deals in no allegories of incarnate deities, but declares as fact, "the Lord was made flesh and dwelt amongst us, and we beheld His glory." It reveals God, not as a blind fate, working concealed behind necessary laws of nature, but God moving up and down in Human History, "doing His pleasure among the armies of heaven, and among the inhabitants of earth." It proclaims an Historical Christ, who lived and wept and died among men, and who now reigns "a Prince and a Saviour at the right hand of the Majesty in the Heavens."

It has a philosophy, indeed, which reason's golden reed shall take an eternity to measure, for the length and the breadth and the height of it are equal; a philosophy, whose depth shall not be plumbed this side the gates of heaven. Yet, as a religion, its basis is the testimony of God, accrediting the facts which are level to the peasant and the sage alike.— Both accept it upon the same grounds, and by the same faith in a divine testimony. Thus Christiani-

ty is competent to be, what Paganism is not, a c
tholic religion for man as man, embracing within i
comprehension, sympathy, and holy fellowship, a
ranks of social condition.

4. I draw your attention next to a point mo
material in this defence: *that Christianity is pr
eminently a religion of law*, and *alone solves the pr
blems which arise from the Holiness and Justice a
Jehovah.*

We cannot conceive of a finite moral being wh
is not, ex vi termini, a subject of law. If he is er
dowed with understanding, conscience and will, h
must be cognizant of duty; and if he is a create
being, his limited faculties require the guidance of
perfect standard of virtue. Angels in Heaven, an
devils in Hell are neither of them exempt from th
jurisdiction of law, simply because they have passe
the bounds of probation. The blessedness of th
one consists in the reward bestowed upon a perfec
and confirmed obedience, as the penalty inflicte
upon continual and hopeless transgression occasior
the misery of the other. No heresy can be mor
glaring or fatal than that of the anti-nomian; wh
not only strikes at the authority of God, but repr
diates also the nature which is given to man, an
utterly destroys the morality of every human a
tion. Here was the capital defect of Pagan theolo
gy. It regarded simply the abstract existence, a

else the natural perfections of the Deity. Its effort was by transcendental speculations to compass the mystery of his being, and then to explain how he can be the author of the material world so alien from his essence. Such inquiries were however rather physical than moral. The infinite purity of His nature formed no part of their conception of God; nor did they recognize a holy and immutable law which should express his claims upon the love and obedience of his subjects. Hence the grand problem of all religion, how God shall be "just and yet justify the ungodly," was never even proposed for solution. If hecatombs smoked on heathen altars, it was to placate the capricious anger of beings who were mighty, rather than to appease the holy wrath of a wise and righteous ruler.

Precisely the same fatal defect vitiates all the fond schemes devised by the Deists of the 17th and 18th centuries, who labored to trick off natural religion and to set her up as the rival of moral Christianity. Whether it be contended—as in one school seduced by a false analogy with human governments—that God may, in the exercise of mere supremacy, remit the penalty of the law and grant a general amnesty to transgressors; or, as in another, that simple repentance is a sufficient ground of Divine forgiveness; or, as in a third, that God may punish sin in part, either in the sufferings of this life or in the purgato-

rial torments of the next; in all alike, the holin
of God is sunk out of view—the law, which from
absolute perfection must be immutable, is cancel
—or else sentence is craftily commuted, by the si
stitution of another penalty than that which orig
ally enforced its claims.

Yet this difficulty, which baffles alike the wisd
of the rationalist and the mystic, Christianity bo.
ly and honestly meets in its doctrine of atoneme
It openly proclaims the unchangeable holiness of t
Divine law; but announces salvation to the sinn
through a perfect satisfaction rendered to its drea
ful curse. It provides a surety for the sinner in t
person of God's Eternal Son; who, being above t
law, owes no obedience for himself; who, havi
infinite resources, is able to endure the Fathe
wrath; who being God, has power to lay down l
life and power to take it again. His Divine subs
tute becomes a true man by supernatural birth
a virgin, and for man passes under the law to e
dure its curse. By legal union with Him, this ol
dience glorious above all other obedience in bei
rendered to both precept and penalty alike, is rec
oned to the beliver as though accomplished by hi
self. And in this righteousness which meets eve
challenge of the law, the sinner is henceforward
quitted and accepted before the Judge. Nor is tl
all. The transgressor's own conscience is purg

from a sense of guilt, and by this reconciliation with the law the very ground is removed upon which all accusations rested. Thus does Christianity build itself upon eternal principles of righteousness and of law; and justice no less than mercy becomes the guarantee of our salvation. Not more surely, Gerizim and Ebal of old echo to each other across the vale of Shechem the blessings and the curses of the Mosaic covenant, than from Calvary to Sinai the fulfilled curse rebounds across a ransomed world. And in the porch of that august temple which Christianity has reared, wherein all nations shall gather to worship, the Justice and the Grace of God shall forever stand, the Jachin and the Boaz, the pillars of stability and strength as well as the glory and the ornament.

5. I ascend another step in reaching to "the height of this great argument," when I say that *Christianity is the only religion which provides for the renovation of our nature, in its doctrine of the new birth.*— Sin has not only deranged our relations to God, but has cut us off from Him who is the only source of the Creature's holiness, corrupting all his nature.— Even supposing reconciliation with law to be effected, how is this new difficulty to be met? Should the sinner by a judicial decree or by the exercise of arbitrary power be elevated to Heaven, the necessary repulsion between his defilement and the Divine

purity would precipitate him even from the steps
the eternal throne, or change the joys of Heaven i
to instruments of torture:

> " —————————From the bottom stirs
> The Hell within him ; for within him hell
> He brings, and round about him, nor irom hell
> One step, no more than from himself, can fly
> By change of place."

What remedy does the intellectual idolatry of th
Deist, or the grosser idolatry of the Pagan, provid
for this exigency ?   Neither the cold ethics of th
one, nor the bloody rites of the other, undertake t
rectify the inward nature of man and to fit it fc
obedience or worship.   Hence communion of sou
with God forms no part of either scheme.   It is a
though a pardon should be brought after the poo
criminal lies cold under the executed sentence of th
law.   The form of a man is there, with all the or
gans perfect and entire, but no more instinct wit
life.   Just here Christianity interposes with its d
vine remedy.   An almighty energy quickens one
more that prostrate form ; and the supple organ
play again, obedient to the mysterious principle o
life, which actuates and moves the whole.   Were
called upon to select a single verse from the Bibl
upon which the last issue of Christianity should b
staked, the oracle of Christ to Nicodemus should b
that pass of Thermopylae where its truth shoul
stand or fall : " Verily, verily, I say unto thee, ex

cept a man be born again, be shall not see the kingdom of God." And with the air of one who is as-
sured of his triumph, I would proclaim the challenge of Isaiah of old: "Assemble yourselves and
come; draw near together, ye that are escaped of
the nations; tell ye and bring them near; yea, let
them take counsel together; who hath declared
this from ancient time? Who hath told it from
that time? Have not I the Lord? and there is no
God else beside me." Ah! this is the glory of the
Gospel, that it reveals the religion of a sinner. It
not only tells of a great propitiatory sacrifice,
smoking ever upon the altar in the outer court,
and proclaiming "without the shedding of blood,
there is no remission of sin;" it not only tells of a
great High Priest within the veil, interceding before the mercy-seat, with hands which never, like
those of Moses, hang down: But it tells of this
almighty Spirit, who comes with a silent, yet re-
sistless power, into the sanctuary of the human soul;
who quickens the sinner dead in tresspasses and
sins, breathing into him a new life of holiness and
love; who pours into his understanding the beams
of light from his own glorious person; who turns
the affections back in their flowing current, till they
empty into the bosom of God; who sways the will
not by an external necessity, but magnetizing it
through the operation of grace, "makes it willing

in the day of his power," so that in its own polar
it points freely to the law of God, and " ev
thought is brought into captivity and obedience
Christ." It tells of the same Spirit, who dwells i
ever within the renewed soul, and brings the n
born nature to maturity of growth ; and finally
tisfies its craving for an immortality of virtue,
translating it to the presence of God, where in i
immediate vision of the Good it is confirmed, li
the angels, indefectibly in holiness. Produce n
form the records of deism or of priestcraft, c
form of religion, which professes to beget the sinr
anew in the holy image of God, and I will be st
gared by a rising doubt ; but until you shall
this,

> " I'll bind the Gospel to my heart,
> And call *them* vanity and lies."

6.—Christianity will set up but one more plea
her defence, *that of being the only system of religio*
to absolute certainty of whose truth it is possible
be brought. By the inward work of God's Spi
upon the soul, in regeneration and sanctification,
the doctrines of revelation are brought within t
range of experience, so as to be confirmed by t
testimony of consciousness. Truth is collected
the Scripture, as light is gathered into the sun.
Yet the sinner's mind, like the eye of the blind,
closed against its rays. If now the Holy Ghost i

moves the veil which has shrouded it in darkness, quickens it enfeebled by sin, renders it congenial with the truth it is to receive, and then without the aid of artificial symbols, so to speak, impresses that truth nakedly upon the mind, there must be a correspondence between the objective revelation on the one hand, and the subjective illumination on the other. Not more certainly does the seal leave its impression upon the softened wax, than do the doctrines of grace upon the believer's heart. There is not one so abstract and unpractical, but it is the type or mould of christian feeling : nor an emotion of the renewed heart, but is awakened by its kindred truth. Is it not obvious that such a system admits a certainty of conviction which is attainable in no other? It is seen not only in the direct light which beams from itself, but in the reflected light of human consciousness. The truths are known, because felt as well as seen. And there was a deep though unsuspected philosophy in the reply of the unlettered peasant to the subtle sceptic: "Sir, I cannot answer your arguments," but, laying her hand on her breast, "I feel here that the Bible is true." We *know* the doctrine of regeneration to be true because we are quickened, who before were dead in sins. We *know* the doctrine of spiritual illumination to be true; for "whereas we were blind, now we see." We *know* union with Christ to be true, be-

cause conscious that we walk by faith in Him. W
know adoption to be true; for the spirit of sons
spread abroad in our hearts, crying Abba, Fathe
We *know* justification by faith to be true; because
we who believe have peace with God, which pa
seth all understanding. Thus we may pass aroun
the entire circle of christian doctrine, and like th
notes marked upon the keys of a well tuned instru
ment, the sanctified heart will give to each its ow
responsive sound. He, who by the teaching of th
Holy Ghost has felt the power of all truth in h
own soul, comes through experience to " the riche
of the full assurance of understanding, to the a
knowledgement of the mystery of God, and of th
Father, and of Christ, in whom are hid all the trea
sures of wisdom and knowledge." While, too, th
written word reproduces itself in the heart of th
Christian, it is the perfect standard by which all th
secret exercises of that heart are to be judged
precisely as in the Photographic art, the light bean
ing from an object draws the image on the plate
while the original remains to test the accuracy c
the resemblance. In this way an important chec
is imposed upon the wayward and licentious tenc
encies of the imagination. The mystic cannot eas
ly mistake his dreams and reveries for the inspira
tions of the Spirit ; for, as He works outwardl
from the scripture upon the mind, we have a lav

and a testimony to which these inspirations can be referred; and if "they be not according to this word, it is because there is no light in them."

It is time, young gentlemen, to pause and see whither the swelling tide of this discussion has drifted us. I have not spoken in vain if you are brought to a practical conviction, that you cannot dispense with all religion. You may select any one of the systems which you shall find ticketed and labelled in the vast museum of history. You may dream among the mystics of India, or divine among the star-gazers of Chaldea. You may sacrifice to the sun upon the hill-tops of ancient Persia, or veil yourselves before the consecrated fire of the Magi. You may wreathe garlands around the sacred Bull of Egypt, or dance with amulets and fetishes among the devil-worshippers of Caffraria; or turning with contempt from these gross and obsolete idolatries; you may echo the profane wit of the French Encyclopedists, or boast in the starched proprieties of intellectual Deism. You may look forth upon this beautiful world and exclaim, in the Pantheistic language of Pope,

> " All are but part of one stupendous whole,
> Whose body nature is, and God the soul:"

or, you may write your own inscriptions upon the altar reared by natural religion to " the unknown God." You may cast aside all the forms of worship and walk the steep path of earthly ambition, wear the thorns with which heroes are crowned; you may go tripping through the world, a devot of pleasure, to the sound of timbrel and harp ; (standing under Heaven's high arch, with your e; upon the stars, you may proclaim in this vast, y vacant temple of Jehovah, "there is no God!". yet still you shall not escape from the imperishab instincts of your religious nature. Crush out as yc may, this element which most allies you to ange and to God, in secret hours you must hear awf; whispers from an oracle within, warning you th; you can only become an apostate from God, by bei; first an apostate from yourself.

I have come from afar to ask you solemnly, whic of these religions do you accept as yours? If yc reply with Peter in the text, to whom shall we ε but to Christ, who has these words of Eternal lif I thank you for the answer; but have you cons dered what is involved in the acceptance of Christ anity? Resting as an historical religion, upon tl testimony of God himself, given in an authentic r velation, it is not to be received by an easy tradit onal faith, as an ancestral heir-loom. To appropr ate an argument of Dr. Chalmers upon the being (God, if Christianity only presents you with a pr sumption of its truth, this binds you to a close an earnest investigation of its evidences, that you ma come to an absolute conviction of that truth. Jehovah is a jealous God, who will not give his glory to another: and He claims this homage of our intellect, that the system of faith of which His veracity is the pledge, should be received only upon that personal conviction which flows from a knowledge of its contents, and an examination of its claims; such a conviction as shall forever exclude even the possible rivalry of other systems. Especially is this demand just upon you, who have here been taught those secrets of nature, which science breathes but to few, and which are the foot-prints of the christian argument for the being of a God.— You who have conversed with Plato in the Academy, and with Zeno in the Porch—you who, with your hands upon the records of learning and philosophy treasured in these archives, are so competent to institute the comparison which I have drawn to-night between the religion of God and of men:— upon you, it is specially incumbent to give in your adhesion to christianity, not upon a traditional and hereditary trust, but upon the faith of the intensest personal conviction.

Remember, too, that Christianity is not to be accepted simply as a philosophy, explaining the otherwise insoluble problems of human life. If it were nothing more than this, the Bible would still deserve to be studied above all the tomes of human

wisdom, under which our bookshelves groan ; for
contains the utterances of Divine wisdom. But t
Gospel reveals not a philosophy which explai
man's wants, but a religion which meets them.
proposes reconciliation with God through an ator
ment which satisfies all the requisitions of law ; al
it renews and sanctifies the soul, fitting it for a
eternal and blissful communion with its Maker,
this world and in that which is to come. If in tl
aspect you accept it, you can only do so by an i
ward experience of its power. Let me impress u
on you this distinction. The Scriptures may be
you only the grove of Academus, and Jesus Chri
but a diviner Socrates.

Initiated in all the mysteries of its philosoph
you may wither and die whilst standing at the vei
fountain of life. Remember, I pray you, that
Christ be a teacher, his are " the words of Etern
Life." You must touch the hem of his garmei
and be healed. You must be sprinkled with H
blood, so as " to have no more conscience of sins
You must have fellowship with him in his deal
and resurrection. You must experience the rene
ing and sanctifying, influences of the Holy Ghos
or, nominally Christian as you may be, you w
sink from the very shadow of the Saviour's cro
into eternal perdition. Young gentlemen, I spe
these words in deep solemnity of soul. Throug

your partial kindness I am here to-night: but I am here as a minister of God, to speak His words upon which the destiny of souls is suspended. This night has the kingdom of God come nigh unto you: and if you receive it not, I say unto you, it shall be more tolerable in that day for Sodom than for you. "If ye were blind, ye should have no sin: but now ye say, we see, therefore your sin remaineth." "But I hope better things of you, and things that accompany salvation, though I thus speak." "To God and to the Spirit of his grace I commend you." May his guardian providence shield you in this life, from sorrow and from sin! and may it be yours and mine to hear together the benediction of the last day, "come ye blessed of my Father, inherit the Kingdom prepared for you from the foundation of the world!"

CPSIA information can be obtained
at www.ICGtesting.com
Printed in the USA
BVHW070818311218
536770BV00013B/242/P